Sagittarius

November 23 — December 21

Thru the Numbers

Sagittarius

November 23 — December 21

by
Paul & Valeta Rice

SAMUEL WEISER, INC.

York Beach, Maine

First published in 1983 by
Samuel Weiser, Inc.
Box 612
York Beach, Maine 03910

Reprinted, 1991

Library of Congress Catalog Card Number: 82-63004

ISBN 0-87728-573-X (Sagittarius)

BJ

Printed in the United States of America

Depending on the year involved, the sun changes
zodiac signs on different days, consequently sources
vary in the dates they give to indicate the change-
over. Those born close to the beginning/end of a
sign are not on the "cusp" as is commonly believed.
There is a clear demarcation. If you are unsure of
your sign you may want to have your chart
calculated—or you can buy both books and see
which one works for you!

Contents

AUTHORS

If Valeta and Paul Rice sound familiar, it may be because of their extensive travel around the United States, from Alaska to the coast of California, from the East coast to Hawaii. During their invitational stopovers, they conducted workshops and seminars about Name Analysis and Birth Analysis. This continued for over twenty years until Paul's death in 1988.

Paul Rice was an engineer and Valeta a minister and psychic counselor. While their professions were very different they shared an interest in occult studies for more than 40 years, which started with their introduction to a book about ESP from Duke University. Their search for esoteric knowledge carried them into astrology, reincarnation, palmistry, tarot, color, music, I Ching, ESP, dream analysis, the qabala, yoga, structural dynamics, meditation/visualization/healing and many more sciences—techniques found both beneficial and rewarding by their clients.

They have also published *Potential: The Name Analysis Book* (Samuel Weiser, 1987) which provides an in-depth look at the special numerological nuances your name holds.

Valeta Rice still holds private consultations and is also available for lectures. She can be contacted at:

Valeta Rice
F.A.C.E. Association
177 Webster Street, #A105
Monterey, CA 93940

WHEN?

When shall I start my next project?
When should I ask for a raise?
When should I sign that contract?
When should I get married?
How will I feel when I retire?

How many times has a person looked for an answer to these questions? During this modern age the veil has been lifted on the ancient science of the vibration of the NUMBERS. This ancient science, known as the *metaphysical science of numerology*, was developed by Pythagoras, who lived in the sixth century B.C.

The simplicity of NUMEROLOGY is astounding. If you can count on your fingers you can use Numerology. It requires only a few hours study before you can begin to put to use the basic facts that you have acquired. This knowledge will give one the opportunity to see himself and other acquaintances in a better light. Apparently its simplicity is the reason Numerology was used less than other occult sciences in the past, and our society today seems to prefer complexity also.

Surprisingly, the knowledge of the numbers which govern your life will reveal many things you already know, that you had suspected or you had hoped were true.

The Numerologist takes his place alongside the Astrologer, Graphologist, Palmist and the Tarot reader, who all believe that we came into this life, not by chance, but by choice, and from these arts or sciences much can be revealed about a person's life.

Numerology reveals the vibrations in many categories including the number connected to the Birth Date, the Personal Year, the Personal Month and how the planet vibrations correlate to these numbers.

The awareness of the numbers connected to these categories helps us with a yearly and monthly course to follow.

6 PAUL AND VALETA RICE

Everyone wants to be happy and prosperous. Many unfortunate people have not learned to harmonize their birthdate vibrations with the timing of their decisions.

We are constantly called upon to make decisions which may make significant changes in our lives. Often we make the wrong decisions over family, friends, or in business because our "TIMING" is off.

The simple system of the vibration of the numbers and how they pertain to your life and the timing of your decisions will help you to come to logically deduced insights and, if carefully followed,will make you increasingly happy and prosperous throughout your lifetime.

Pythagoras, who lived twenty-five centuries ago, is considered the Father of Numbers. It is believed that he received his knowledge of the occult value of the numbers while in Egypt and Babylon. He taught these concepts and many more in his School of Occult Philosophy where the few who were allowed to attend learned how "everything can be related to numbers."

The Science of Numerology is not a quick way to happiness and achievement; it is only by becoming aware of your favorable number vibrations and then changing the unfavorable vibrations that you can smooth your pathway.

Numbers live and numbers tell and everyone can become aware of their vibrations and their relationship to themselves through the numbers.

We have explored the mundane and esoteric values of the numbers and their relationship to astrology with a lot of help from our guides.

This knowledge we wish to share with you.

SAGITTARIUS

November 23rd to December 21st   MUTABLE/FIRE

The CENTAUR   *Ruler: JUPITER*

Friendly, gifted, lucky Sagittarius! Your energy flows outward and upward into the future, reaching for more enlightenment as you sometimes leave physical duties behind. If you feel guilty about not getting the house clean or your desk cleared, you could become more and more frustrated with your unfinished cycles. This frustration can lead to blaming others for your inability to handle all the exciting adventures you wish to explore.

"If you would hit the mark, you must aim a little above it," Longfellow says. And, Sagittarius, you do just that, aiming higher and higher, reaching for the stars, the promise of fulfillment. And fulfillment you receive, for you work at it; when one goal is reached you strive for another. No matter what trophies you bring home you always know that you can do better the next time.

Your wit and drive usually brings you to the winner's circle and those who have not been hurt by your careless (and well-meaning) remarks applaud your successes.

It is hard for you to remain in one position or one place for long, especially inside a house; you long for the freedom of the outdoors, the beach, the meadows and anywhere you can be surrounded with lots of space.

In mythology Hercules had to perform twelve labors. In his seventh labor, the Centaur (representative of man emerging from his animal self) shot his arrow at the attacking birds. These birds represented the last vestiges of man's little personality which held him back. Man was set free to expand into his true spiritual self.

It is hard to catch you Sagittarians and hold you in marriage; you prefer to do the galloping after your love. You are a sunny, open-countenanced person who is truthful. You can play the clown or the knight astride a white horse; or use your clever wit to pin your lovers to the mat with plain talk on imperfections (your mates').

PARTNERS: Don't tell a Sagittarian—ask. They do not take to being bossed—yet they like a firm hand on the reins of love and marriage. Wishy-washy lovers and mates are not for Sagittarians; they pull well in double harness when they realize they have to pull together.

JUPITER: Is known as the planet of benevolence, idealism, compassion, generosity and optimism. It showers the good things on all within Sagittarius' range. Sometimes extravagant and self-indulgent; turning to cynicism when frustrated and negative.

MUTABLE: This is the Sagittarius aspect of force manifesting in matter. This indicates flexibility, changeableness, openness to suggestion, interest in people, involvement in personal relationships. The joiner scattering forces; the worrier.

FIRE: These are the virtues brought forth from former lifetimes. They are energy, enthusiasm, wisdom, understanding, inspiration and joy of living.

NEGATIVE VIBRATIONS: Direct as an arrow and sometimes as hurtful, they say things in a way that injures another's self-image, then try to remedy this by saying what was really meant and getting their feet as crossed up as a horse who has run into barbed wire. Sagittarians do not really mean to hurt, it just comes out of their mouths that way; then they are astonished that the person took it the wrong way and try their best to make it up to them.

NUMBERS: The NUMBERS connected to Sagittarius' BIRTH SIGN increases or decreases Sagittarius' energy. Wherever you find Sagittarius in your chart look at the influence your DESTINY NUMBER has on this house in your horoscope.

HOW TO COMPUTE YOUR DESTINY

Your DESTINY, sometimes called the LIFE PATH, is the road that you as an individual travel. This is why you are here, what you should be doing in this lifetime in order to fulfill your soul. The NUMBER combined with your SAGITTARIUS BIRTH SIGN reveals your soul urge, your reason for incarnating this lifetime. If you do not follow your DESTINY, you can become frustrated with unresolved goals.

Each month is represented by a number:

JANUARY	1	APRIL	4	JULY	7	OCTOBER	1
FEBRUARY	2	MAY	5	AUGUST	8	NOVEMBER	2
MARCH	3	JUNE	6	SEPTEMBER	9	DECEMBER	3

Write your BIRTHDATE on your PERSONAL CHART, page 26, using the NAME of your month—NOVEMBER or DECEMBER—not the number of the month. Be sure to use the full year, i.e., 1935, *NOT* '35; or 1940, *NOT* '40, or whatever is the year of your birth. We use the "1" in the year, i.e., 1935, 1966, 1940, as well as the rest of the numbers.

On scratch paper add the number of the month, the day of the month and the year of your birth together, then reduce this number by constantly adding the numbers together until you come to a single digit or a MASTER NUMBER.

The MASTER NUMBERS are **11, 22, 33, 44, 55** and **66.**

EXAMPLE:	Dec.	9,	1944($1944 = 1 + 9 + 4 + 4 = 18; 1 + 8 = 9$)
	3	9	9 $= 21; 2 + 1 =$ **3**
EXAMPLE:	Dec.	5,	1961
	3	5	8 $= 16; 1 + 6 =$ **7**
EXAMPLE:	Dec.	10,	1953($1 + 9 + 5 + 3 = 18; 1 + 8 = 9$)
	3	10	9 $=$ **22** or **4**

Experiment with your birthdate and see if you can come up with a "hidden" MASTER NUMBER.

We call this third example *Research and Discovery* since we have found a *hidden* Master Number. When the Master Numbers are hidden an unexpected talent lies in the direction of the vibration of that particular number.

EXAMPLE: December 12, 1962 = 3 (December) + 12 (the day) + 18 (1 + 9 + 6 + 2) = **33.** Then 3 + 3 = **6** so we write this birthdate **33/6** and look up both numbers to see the level this person is operating on.

So, Sagittarius, every time you find a **1, 2, 4, 6** or **8** in your birth sign or someone else's birth sign try all these methods. Then you find out if you or another person is vibrating on the Master Number or the single digit. There are persons who are content to vibrate and work on the single digit pulsation and put their talents to excellent use in that position rather than try for the esoteric vibration of the Master Numbers. This depends a lot on other numbers which concern several other categories in numerology.

The main purpose of finding your DESTINY NUMBER is to realize where you are in life's stream and learn to flow with it.

The DESTINY NUMBER and your BIRTH SIGN are two things that you cannot change. You were born on a certain day, month, and year, for you chose to be here at that time to experience what you have come to this lifetime to learn.

Another way to research and discover if you have a hidden Master Number is to add this way:

December 10, 1934 = 3 + 10 + 19 + 34 = **66** or **3**
December 8, 1914 = 3 + 8 + 19 + 14 = **44** or **8**
November 28, 1906 = 2 + 28 + 19 + 06 = **55** or **1**

The following pages will interpret the number you have chosen to go with your birth sign for this lifetime.

DESTINY NUMBER 1

In your search for enlightenment you surge ahead taking every course, seminar to which you have access, to find the answers to your intelligent questions. Did we mention your library? Stacks of reference and "how to" books to keep you informed. Your enthusiasm and creativity is at its highest in this number.

Your search for knowledge is insatiable in whatever field your interest lies. Create, invent, design, and conceive the untried. 1 gives you the impetus to do this. You may not have the stability or the interest to finish what you started, but that is okay as you can turn the job over to a 4 or 2 Cancer or Taurus and they will complete it for you. A 9 Virgo will even do it with love.

Find some time for yourself as you reach out in your meditation and relaxation period for these fresh ideas. Your higher mind will assist you to open the channels.

Emotionally you are on fire with your ambitions. You even plunge into romantic entanglements with a recklessness that stops just short of commitment to a life-long partnership. Catching you for a mate is like lassoing a wild horse (the centaur). You just don't want to be penned and unable to roam the field at will. However, once you are caught (with love and sincere attention) you usually remain loyal, for to negate your choice of a mate is to deny your own intelligent selection of a partner. You did want to start a permanent relationship, didn't you? Your arrow (Cupid's this time) found its mark.

NEGATIVE: This is arrogance, knowing more than your peers and letting them know how you feel. It is not deliberate, it just slips out in your conversation; you have the answers to everything! You really do not mean to be bossy or tyrannical, it is just that you have all these books and "they" say to do this or that.

Number 1

Color: Red—for energy. Project this to others.
Element: Fire—more energy. Take your vitamins.
Musical Note: C—the self-starter.

DESTINY NUMBER 2

Your creative mind has a rare quality that detects the truth underlying the lies in others' statements. People can be lying deliberately and you will be more than willing to "set them straight." If they are lying subconsciously you can carefully lead them into revealing their true feelings.

This is the mark of the excellent psychologist or counselor if you can recognize this in yourself. A lot of patience is needed to listen to the tales of others. You would much rather be roaming the glades and forests of nature than be roaming in other people's minds for any lengthy period.

The patience that this number gives you subdues the fire of your ambitions so you can work with other people and their ideas. Cooperative, rhythmic, peaceable and patient are adjectives you can assign to yourself. You can become the diplomat who affects compromises between countries or individuals, providing you do not get careless in your speech and attitude.

This Destiny Number will help you retain your cool with your family and friends when your ideas or your discipline is questioned. Your mate or love will soon learn not to push you too far as your temper when unleashed is something to behold.

NEGATIVE: It will be hard to sublimate your Sagittarius ego in order to work in harness with others. Being overly sensitive about yourself can turn objective criticisms into personal affronts. Don't delude yourself about your importance or you will become covertly hostile, a feeling which can only be suppressed so long.

Number 2

Color: Orange—for balance and peace.
Element: Water—dealing in and with emotions.
Musical Note: D—for peace and tranquility, soothing the fevered brow of discontent.

DESTINY NUMBER 3

This is one of the best Destiny Numbers for Sagittarius, as it emphasizes the good fellowship, the love of entertaining and the gathering of friends and family. Your democratic attitude brings you friends from every walk of life. You are usually surrounded by princes and paupers, neither compromising your love of freedom. You treat them both alike.

On the serious side, you have the potential of becoming a counselor because of your intuitive ability. 3s are willing to contend with other people's vibrations in order to bring them to a better understanding of themselves and their attitudes. You can use drama and comedy to get your ideas across, as well as the use of analogies or the retelling of some of your own experiences that can help others understand their own problems.

Communication is the keyword for 3s. The combination of the 1 of creativity with the 2 of diplomacy leads to communicating on a very high level of understanding, Sagittarius. Learn how to interpret your dreams and elevate yourself by paying attention to their lessons.

3s can pick up the vibrations of those around them, act as a catalyst, and then project these ideas and vibrations to other people through their ability to amuse and entertain. This is the number of the extrovert, one who appreciates a little applause.

You love and give much attention to others. Your mate or lover should appreciate your efforts to hold everything together with love and humor.

NEGATIVE: Guard against overacting. Since you have the ability to pick up the rays of others make sure you shine on your own personality. Watch that you do not "take over" the spotlight and invalidate others' talents.

Number 3

Color: Yellow—for expression.
Element: Fire—for energy.
Musical Note: E—for healing.

DESTINY NUMBER 4

Your concentration is on security during this lifetime, Sagittarius. Your financial protection will come through hard work and focusing on your ultimate goals. There is potential success and achievement in this number if and when you put your energies into whatever you decide is your life's work. Application of your energies is important even though Jupiter is ready to give you the blessing of abundance.

Find a profession that you enjoy in order to get the most out of this lifetime; no need to go grubbing along in a job that you hate. Since you want freedom and independence and are willing to work hard to attain these two goals, choose wisely and think of your "work" as your play time. You could rise to the top of your profession if you take the objective viewpoint—look at your job from a bird's eye view and get an overall picture of where you are going and what you are going to do about it. You are willing to keep "your nose to the grindstone" if you see that promotions are possible and rewards are coming.

This number is loyalty personified, being ready to adjust to your mate's wishes provided he/she will listen to "your" side of the story.

4 is also the number of manifestation. You can make your goals and purposes happen in your lifetime.

Should you become interested in the healing professions, use your hands to inject this healing energy in massage, holistic healing or reflexology.

NEGATIVE: Rigid opinions and inflexibility is the trap of this number. Relax a little; unbend.

Number 4

Color: Beautiful, healing green.
Element: Earth—the stable person.
Musical Note: F—for construction, the builder.

DESTINY NUMBER 5

Most Sagittarians love the freedom of movement, moving from one place to another, and this number emphasizes this quality. This number unsticks you from the mundane occupations, the ordinary jobs which are uninteresting to your restless nature. Your sociable nature would be happiest in positions where you would meet and deal with many people. You can become easily bored with routine, preferring changing scenes, different people and jobs which provide a variety of experiences.

This is a sensual number, giving you more than one love affair, which you handle very nicely, thank you. And your mate or lover will be a person who keeps your interest. Sometimes your need will cause you concern and heartache, yet you cannot complain about being bored. It is change that you are interested in. Try a Scorpio **5** or an Aries **3** if you want challenge and adventure. These two signs and numbers can keep you guessing. Frustrating isn't it, when you are seeking freedom?

If you think of all the numbers which have led up to **5**— the creativity of **1**, the diplomacy of **2**, the intuition of **3**, and the loyalty of **4**, you have an overview of the essence of life itself, giving you the CHOICE of many directions.

NEGATIVE: If you are now leading a monotonous life take a careful scrutiny at the past years to discover where you took the particular path that you now tread. You can change your vocation, your attitudes, and your environment to get out of this rut. What do you really want?

Number 5

Color: Turquoise—like a refreshing breeze blowing away the cobwebs of your mind.
Element: Air—the breath of life.
Musical Note: G—denoting change.

DESTINY NUMBER 6

Self-realization is possible since you have access to the doorway of your higher mind. Love opens the door and **6**'s energy flows forth to encompass those around them. You enclose your family and friends in arms of love and caring, Sagittarius.

This love can be used to bring in the healing vibrations that can be sent out to those who are in need of balancing their body. Healing takes place when the patient understands the cause of the discomfort and is willing to change his attitude toward the cause.

Your understanding of human nature can help you settle disputes and bring harmony to relationships. Your attention to minutiae and your intelligent observation of people and circumstances could equip you for positions in some type of personnel work. You are or could become a judge, reporter, nurse, physician or educator. These suggestions are only potentials; other numbers in your chart would point accurately to your abilities.

The rough spots in your life can be glided over by applying your spontaneous wit and humor, though sometimes people laugh at your inept jokes because they love you. Do you usually get the punch line?

NEGATIVE: All this love and caring can turn into interfering where you are not asked or wanted. The cosmic mother that you represent in a **6** wants to take care of everyone and most people want to learn to do their own tasks and make their own mistakes. Your relationships with your loved ones can be intense at times, both positive and negative, yet it is usually of short duration. Your fire sign burns brightly like a sky rocket but briefly. Your mutable sign flows gently downstream until it hits a hot rock of frustration, then watch the steam rise!

Number 6

Color: Royal blue—for stability; meditate on this color.
Element: Earth—responsibility to self and others.
Musical Note: *A*—for receptivity, harmony.

DESTINY NUMBER 7

7, the symbol of the search for metaphysical knowledge, brings the Sagittarian to a high point of intelligent questing for inner wisdom. Sagittarians must find out about the mysteries of life and beyond, or they will be unhappy in this Destiny. There are so many theories to explore, so many paths to travel and so many ways to study the experience they go through.

You can become the mystic working with and through other people to discover what makes us all tick, why we react to different stimuli. Your conclusions, uttered with truthful abandon, can anger or correct the recipient of your advice. Truth is not that easy to accept for most of us, Sagittarius.

For yourself, look inward at your motivations. Are you "helping" others for your own self-satisfaction or are you doing all this work in order to help others? If it is sincerely to help others, you also will receive the reward.

7s are the bridge from the known to the unknown, from the mundane to the esoteric. Sometimes they even have to build their own bridge to get where they want to be.

Give love and joy to your mate or lover and your family. Love begets love. Your inner wisdom will tell you when the right person comes along to share with you.

NEGATIVE: An overwhelming amount of knowledge floods your brain making you want to hide. You may want to boast and brag about how much you know. Remaining aloof for awhile will give you space to get your act together. The lowest vibration of this number is to suppress knowledge or suppress people and keep them from succeeding in their vocation.

Number 7

Color: Violet—for reverence.
Element: Water—for reflection, mirroring your attitudes.
Musical Note: *B*—for reflection.

DESTINY NUMBER 8

This is the number of prosperity, Sagittarius. Choose your weapons, fame—glory—power—or even money! Use these vibrations wisely. Money—the acquisition of, the handling of, and the spending of—can bring happiness and it can bring harm; it depends entirely on your attitude toward your prosperity.

Large corporations need **8**s to organize and delegate positions of authority to others so that the wheels of commerce keep moving. You have an intelligent mind, Sagittarius, and you can use this ray to determine your direction in life, no matter what your earthly age. Think carefully about your future so that your plans and your goals have meaning and purpose as you move forward in your chosen path.

You can be the head of large corporations, deal in business and industry or go into government positions of power. Watch your verbal goofs as you forge ahead. You don't mean to hurt anyone, you are programmed to tell the truth. And the truth will make you free, say the sages; sometimes it can free you from your job or position and put you out in the cold. However, Sagittarius, you would rather be right and truthful than sacrifice your ideals.

Your fire sign is heaped with burning coals of ambition in this number and Jupiter will offer many rewards for your dedication to your true purposes.

Another side to this number is opening or reopening your third eye to the revelation of your spiritual side to gain power over yourself. You can pass on love and vitalness of soul to others.

NEGATIVE: If you discover you can sway, coerce or pummel others into going your way—against their principles—your ego will get away from you and occlude your prosperity. Become a greedy, grasping person and you lose all you gained in this lifetime. You would make a great con-artist as you love to scheme on this negative level.

Number **8**

Color: Rose—the color of love.
Element: Earth—for achievement, material gain.
Musical Note: High *C*—for striving.

DESTINY NUMBER 9

You are truly in your element with this number of brotherly love, Sagittarius. You chose to serve mankind this lifetime and free yourself from personal restrictions. This is the number of the true humanitarian if you wish to follow the path of serving.

Think of **9** as being a combination of all the single digit vibrations: the creativity of **1**, the diplomacy of **2**, the courage of **3**, the loyalty of **4**, the variety of **5**, the nurturing of **6**, the inner wisdom of **7**, and the power of **8**. All these vibrations, used with love, can change the human race, elevating it to a higher dimension of thought and action.

Your Destiny is to deal with people, to serve them in whatever profession you select. Counsel them, encourage them, help them and use your gifts of communication to bring compassion and love to them.

This emotional drain will not be as drastic as it can be in other signs because your ruler, Jupiter, is the planet of benevolence and mercy. However, it is always good to remember that you also need strokes to balance your polarity—give some—get some.

You can also become overly generous with your money and your time.

NEGATIVE: When dealing with those in trouble the trap is becoming a "do gooder" who begins to look with scorn at those unable to handle their own lives. Your friendliness can keep you from the trap of selfishness. The lowest expression of this number is immorality and bitterness.

Number **9**

Color: Yellow-gold—for perfection, the desire to make everything perfect in love.
Element: Fire—for warmth. People gravitate toward you for comfort.
Musical Note: High *D*—for accomplishment, the finishing of your projects.

DESTINY NUMBER 11

This is the first MASTER NUMBER after all the single digits from **1** through **9**. All Master Numbers carry a responsibility, for they are higher vibrations of the single digit to which they reduce, **11** = 1 + 1 or **2**. So **11** should be written **11/2** to show that a person could be vibrating on either or both levels. This holds true for all the MASTER NUMBERS.

This idealistic number taps the subconscious that holds the dream of perfection that is now and is to be, Sagittarius. Your native intelligence can build the confidence that you need between the idea and the realization of the dream.

The centaur aims his arrow high, seeking the target of fulfillment of his goals. Many of your concepts are foreign to the doubters of life and living so you gallop over these skeptical evaluations, racing to your goal line, the mark you have set for yourself. Then holding your trophy high you seek other commitments. This could mean crossing the goal line into another kind of game. Or it could mean turning your back on your successes to seek a new meaning to life.

Your inner flashes of intuition could light the path for many to follow in the material and in the spiritual world.

Your constant search for the perfect mate or lover is difficult as perfection is seldom in the physical, mental and emotional package. We all have our little habits that are leftovers from former lifetimes.

NEGATIVE: Your search for perfection can turn you into a fanatic if you fail to see the reality of the nature of the human race. Each person is working toward whatever goal he has set for himself. **11**s are intuitively brilliant, their goals inspiring; however, their fame can overwhelm them if it turns to greed and self-superiority.

Number **11**

Color: Silver—for attraction.
Element: Air—for the idealistic dream.
Musical Note: High E—for magnetism, the drawing together of people and ideas.

DESTINY NUMBER 22

The year 1984, which reduces to a **22**, will see a rebirth of love and order. **22** is the practical and physical master who has control over his own destiny as it applies to the material world, Sagittarius. You have the idealism of **11** plus the ability to put your dreams into action.

Your international direction could put you into the highest offices in the nation. You have the opportunity to make significant contributions that would reshape the shadows of things to come in politics, government, industry and art.

In order to fulfill this powerful destiny you need to think big, act big and move into the inner circles of power in whatever country you choose. Everyone sincerely hopes that you use this power to help mankind.

You may try to exert this mastery over your mate or lover, so watch it! Look at the challenge a mate who does not always agree with you can give you. A submissive mate is passe in this day and age, Sagittarius.

22 reduces to **4** for those who are not ready for this heady vibration, yet **4** is a manifesting number, getting you what you want. **4** is also known as the work number and work is your middle name, Sagittarius. You can turn work into play as you put your ideas into motion.

There is power here over your physical body to heal yourself. You really do not have time to be sick anyway; life is too exciting to bother with bed, unless bed has more interesting facets.

Choose an intelligent mate or lover or you will be frustrated as you climb upward.

NEGATIVE: Follow through with your great plans or you will become known as the big talker not the big doer. Reach further than your fellow man or you might become frustrated.

Number **22**

Color: Red-gold—for practical wisdom.
Element: Water—for cleansing.
Musical Note: High F—for physical mastery.

DESTINY NUMBER 33

Being or becoming the emotional master, which this number represents, requires study of the emotions. There are many books and philosophies which can enlighten you, Sagittarius. Wander the bookstores and the libraries and be aware of the book titles which seem to jump out at you. Buy or borrow these books and study their content to see what your guides are trying to get across to you.

As you find yourself understanding emotions and where they come from, you will also find yourself evaluating yourself and others. Just don't be too harsh on yourself. Remember that you are in a learning process.

Think of **33** as being the combination of the **11** (the idealist) and **22** (the practical master). This means that you can put your idealism to work in a very practical, logical way that others will understand. You can acquire or already have the patience to be the counselor who understands about the human foibles and how to evaluate these emotional tones. See the advanced section of our book, NAME ANALYSIS, which delineates how the mind and emotions affect a person.

Use your wit and humor to soften the emotional blows struck in anger and frustration. Enthusiasm for your work, your loves, your family or your private life can fire others with the desire to make this world a better place in which to live.

NEGATIVE: If you try to control others with the whip of emotions, you can fall into the trap of revealing your own hidden fears, which could erupt at the moment that you least expect. A soft answer turneth away wrath. A factual answer to an accusation leaves your accuser in a state of jello. Why not try it?

Number **33**

Color: Deep sky-blue—for intensity. Your feelings are on the surface and show in your actions.

Element: Water—for emotional mastery, flowing with or controlling the stream of consciousness.

Musical Note: High G—for emotional healing. Heal emotions, don't excite them into performing evil. When we are triggered into minus emotions by fear, anxiety or grief we are open to suggestion. Suggest the positive solutions to problems.

DESTINY NUMBER 44

This number of the mental master colors your Sagittarian nature. You can bring abundance to your co-workers by using the good sense and intelligence that you chose for this lifetime.

Intelligence (the ability to learn and know) uses logic in this number to point out our mental processes. Logic is a product of our mental processes. There is two-valued logic (right, wrong), three-valued logic (right, wrong and maybe), then there is simply your side, my side and the correct side. If we take a quantum jump we get to infinite-valued logic, "righter" at one time than another or "wronger" at one time than another—infinite distance on either side. You have the ability to choose any of these logical processes since you can handle different levels of consciousness at one time. People may think that you are drifting off into fantasy as your eyes glaze, however, you are only pulling in the different levels of perception in order to solve the immediate problem.

Your mate or lover may find this a hard vibration to handle unless he/she has power of his/her own which matches the desire to succeed. Compromise will be necessary with such a mate. Subservient lovers may seem peaceful at first but you need the challenge of winning (sometimes) over an able person.

44 is a combination of **11** (idealism) and **33** (emotional mastery). **44** is also a double **22**, the physical master, power over self. **44** can stand alone as the powerful manifesting number on the material side. How about the law, medicine or some healing science?

NEGATIVE: There is the inherent threat of rigidity in this number, the attitude that "I am always right because I am always right." Sometimes the negative side shows through by trying to twist the ideas of others to gain fame and fortune.

Number **44**

Color: Blue-green—tranquilizing.
Element: Earth—for mental mastery.
Musical Note: High *A*—for mental healing.

DESTINY NUMBER 55

One way to reach the enlightenment you have been searching for is to spread the awareness and knowledge you have. Share all this with your friends. When we have reached this number, we have the potential of giving life energy, rejuvenation, to ourselves and others if this is done with love.

Reinforce your friends' positive attitudes by paying attention to them. If you reward them with complaints they will drift away.

Think of **55** as being a combination of **22**, the practical master, and **33**, the emotional master. When emotions are controlling you, think of how you can be logical about the situation and breathe life into the solution. Count to three, take a deep breath and look around to see if all this is real when you are faced with a problem.

You are of great value to your community and can go far as a religious teacher, educator, reformer or writer, or any profession which takes you into areas of need so you can lift people out of depression. Your wit, humor and general friendliness make inroads into these areas of suffering.

You can also think of **55** as being a combination of **11**, the idealist, and **44**, the mental master. The idealist wants everything perfect and the mental master can help bring order to a project.

55 is the one who injects life into a project, can handle the upsets and emotions which occur while the job is going on, and on the side teaches those around about friendship and loyalty.

NEGATIVE: Everything said about **1** Destiny Number also applies to a **55**, both positive and negative. The Master Number has the power to move people around and get them to thinking a certain way, regardless if it is right or wrong. Be careful about invalidating anyone, this would just bring on karma.

Number **55**

Color: Red-violet—for life energy.
Element: Air—for spirituality.
Musical Note: Chord of G—for spiritual healing.

DESTINY NUMBER 66

Use the Research and Discovery method, page 10, to see if this powerful Master Number is hidden in your birthdate, Sagittarius. **66** is love energy, the full realization that one cannot love others until he loves himself and can outpour this feeling to others.

66 is truly the cosmic mother vibration, the double six leading to the 9 (6 × 6 = 36; 3 + 6 = 9) which is brotherly love for all mankind. We are not talking about sex, although that is an important part of lovingess, we are referring to the ecstasy that comes over us sometimes in meditation, giving us the feeling that we are truly connected with the cosmos, the Oneness.

Jupiter, the vibration of optimism and generosity, and your fire sign bring energy and enthusiasm and love to a roomful of people. They gravitate toward you as if you were a magnet. You can sway their opinions toward your way of thinking, so be careful how you handle this power. State your own opinions (as opinions) and then be unafraid to march with those who are seeking justice and equality.

NEGATIVE: A negative **66** would gather many people into his camp selling them on the idea that "this is the only way to be saved." They would use the love energy to enslave others, make them do things "in love" that go against our moral codes. Another negative vibration is repressing love for self and for others, keeping family and friends chained to you with "You don't love me enough."

Number **66**

Color: Ultra-rose—the fullest expression of love on this planet. Meditate on this color, it will fully open your heart chakra if all the other laws are followed which have led you to this initiation.

Element: Fire—for burning away the dross.

Musical Note: Any chord struck in harmony. This sound can change the cells in your body if promoted with love.

YOUR PERSONAL CHART

Birthdate _____

Birth Number_____

Birth Sign_____

Birth Element_____

This planetary aspect represents the moral excellence and
goodness that the soul has achieved in former lifetimes, virtues
which will assist a person in this lifetime.

Birth Musical Note_____

Personal Year for 1991_____

Personal Year for 1992_____

Personal Year for 1993_____

Personal Year for 1994_____

Personal Year for 1995_____

Personal Year for 1996_____

Personal Year for 1997_____

Personal Year for 1998_____

Personal Month Numbers:

January _____	July_____
February _____	August _____
March _____	September_____
April _____	October _____
May _____	November _____
June _____	December _____

Challenges:

Major_____

1st   Sub-challenge_____

2nd   Sub-challenge_____

PERSONAL YEAR

The PERSONAL YEAR NUMBER is the vibration that influences your life in any given year. This is a fine focus of JUPITER, the planet of benevolence and idealism. Jupiter showers you with all the good things of life as long as you recognize what the good things are. If you are operating on the negative side of Jupiter, it could lead you into extravagance and greediness.

To obtain this number you add your BIRTH MONTH and your BIRTH DAY to the year you are seeking. For example: If your birth date is December 3, 1961, and you want to find the PERSONAL YEAR for 1981 you do this:

Add 3 (December) to 3 (the day) to 1981 = 1987,
1967 = 1 + 9 + 6 + 7 = 23; 2 + 3 = **5**, the PERSONAL YEAR for the year 1981 for the birth date of December 3, 1961.

Do not use your own birth year; use the year in which you wish to find your PERSONAL YEAR.

PERSONAL MONTH

Still under the influence of that great planet, JUPITER, we also find our own PERSONAL MONTH by adding our PERSONAL YEAR to the current month or the month we are seeking.

For example: December 3, 1961 is the birth date. We want to find the PERSONAL MONTH for AUGUST 1981. Since we have already established the PERSONAL YEAR for this birth date for 1981 as **5**, we simply take the **5** and add it to the month of August which is **8**.

5 (Personal Year) ± **8** (August) = 13; 1 + 3 = **4**. Therefore, the PERSONAL MONTH for the birth date of December 3, 1961 is **4** for August 1981.

Compute your PERSONAL MONTHS and find the interpretations on the following pages.

TABLE OF PERSONAL MONTHS

JUPITER: EXPANSION, UNDERSTANDING, FRIENDLINESS, ABUNDANCE, INSPIRATION, INCREASE, SPUR.

The definitive words for Jupiter listed above captured the essence of the positive side of Jupiter's vibrations. Understand these words by using a good dictionary as you discover the true meaning for yourself. Meditating on all the descriptive words given in this booklet will assist you also.

The NEGATIVE side of the JUPITER vibration is: EXTRAVAGANCE, INDULGENCE, CYNICISM, GREED.

When we talk about the TIMING of your decisions we need to remember that Jupiter has an influence as well as the vibration of the number that you find for your own PERSONAL MONTH. The interpretations for personal months are as follows:

PERSONAL MONTH 1

This is the month to use the Jupiter influence of inspiration to create the kinds of things that you want for the next few months, Sagittarius. You can create material objects or new ideas and plans for the future. We all need this impetus to jar us out of our complacent ruts and give us new and exciting jobs, lovers, friends and challenges. Your fire sign helps motivate you to new endeavors and shoot your arrow straight for the stars. The air is alive with visions as well as music. Be aware of what is going on around you. Always compare your Destiny Number with your birth month number to see how the vibrations compare or conflict. When you understand these vibrations, it is easier to work within the structure.

NEGATIVE: It is very easy for you to express your knowledge to others, your plans and your dreams. Overwhelming others with creative ideas could turn them off, instead of seeing the enthusiastic person you really are, they might see a braggart. Indecisiveness, bossiness and ill-will this month could cause a lot of trouble in the office.

PERSONAL MONTH 2

Time to go dancing, Sagittarius, and relax from the work-a-day world. You get tied into doing for others and need a few strokes yourself. It takes a lot of patience to handle family, business and the hobbies you so enjoy. Friends are always interrupting you, for they know you care about them. Sometimes you just want to be yourself. This sensitivity to your friends and family gives your love somewhere to go for they need you. If they did not need you, you would feel like you had been cheated. This month may include some emotional problems that have to be settled. Don't get too sensitive about yourself. Next month will be a lot better for you.

NEGATIVE: Just keep your cool and become the peacemaker; be the one who brings the warring factions together and provides the calm atmosphere for compromises. Move in perfect rhythm to the sounds of peace.

PERSONAL MONTH 3

Now you can go forward, and if you haven't spilled any milk (of human kindness) last month you can realize some of your dreams. Communicate, don't let others withdraw from you; find out what makes people tick. You have the ability to get to the bottom of any dispute with your friendly outgoing love. This is the month to entertain. Jupiter is right with you. Use your charm and trust in your own abilities. This is also a good month to display your talents, to be seen and heard. It is easy for you to learn since you work from inspiration and intuition.

NEGATIVE: Exaggeration and gossip is the bug-a-boo of the month. The temptation is there to be intolerant of others. Watch your pennies and don't waste your money, your time or your talents.

PERSONAL MONTH 4

This is the Destiny Number that gives you the impetus to be orderly, filing your papers correctly, aligning your spices and canned goods in their proper storage places and in general keeping your surroundings looking good, Sagittarius. Orderliness is somethig you have grown into slowly because there are so many interesting things to delve into that there is little time to categorize everything. The household managers begin to organize their work when they abandon temporary living quarters and move into their own home. Why fix up someone else's house? You will just have to move sooner or later and leave that repaired ceiling, those painted cupboards. This attitude holds true with your job or profession. When you make it your responsibility, you become organized. Remain loyal to your commitments this month. Stay with your job or your family until all the facts relating to the disagreement are in. Duty will overrule the need to find a more comfortable space.

NEGATIVE: You could become violently angry if someone questions your loyalty. You could also become rigid in your opinions to the exclusion of facts.

PERSONAL MONTH 5

This period of change is right up your alley, Sagittarius. You like adventure and new happenings. Of all the signs, you and Gemini like to juggle a few balls in the air at one time. This can be a fun month of travel. We travel on boats, planes and trains and we also travel in our minds to many different spaces and times. Here is the essence of life and living. This is creative mind on the mental level, seeking new avenues of discovery, playing with ideas of invention and using imagination to promote concepts that improve your product. Take time out to let your visualization come through. A little imagination with your mate or lover could bring interesting results.

NEGATIVE: You could become sloppy in your dress, in your speech and with your friends. Inconsistency could lead to self-indulgence in food and drink.

PERSONAL MONTH 6

This is the month to exercise good judgement in all your affairs: business and love. It is also a month for attention to family, giving love and understanding to your mate and children (if any). Communicate your wishes and listen to their wishes so you can come to an agreement about important matters. Many things can be done that concern harmony, like redecorating your home or redesigning your wardrobe. Listen to yourself when you speak, and see if you are really using the word patterns you desire; are you using love or are you just talking to keep the air filled with words? You need human contact, Sagittarius, especially this month. Cuddle up to your family if they will let you and bring harmonious relations closer. Get your strokes by being loving or indulging in your favorite hobbies.

NEGATIVE: You could be interfering in private business of your family where you are not wanted. We love our mates and children and even have concern about our business relationships and do not want to see anyone hurt by wrong decisions. However, it is the prerogative of each of us to make our own mistakes.

PERSONAL MONTH 7

Use your inner wisdom to see the problems that face you then use your outgoing friendliness to bridge the gap from misunderstandings to solutions. You always seek the truth, Sagittarius, and in seeking you will be moving toward your goals and purposes. You have nothing to hide, you are right there, up front. Other people trust you because they see this in you. 7 is always the bridge from the known to the unknown and your direct way of dealing with the things that you want to discover will uncover the knowledge you wish to gain. This number gives you freedom to experiment on many different levels of consciousness and subconsciousness if you keep on the positive side of this number.

NEGATIVE: You could become confused if you are trying to balance too many problems.

PERSONAL MONTH 8

Your Sagittarian luck works directly and indirectly. For instance, when you aim your arrow toward your goal it flies straight and true. Then again if the vibrations are not right for you the arrow misses the target—now wait a minute—if you missed the target today perhaps it is because tomorrow is the lucky day for you to get what you want. That letter you were supposed to mail is still in your possession and while you are feeling guilty, the stock you were going to buy took a nose dive—saving you thousands of dollars. If you just flow with what is happening you will be right there when the money is falling around you this month. Good month for a raise, winning something and being successful in your undertakings. On the esoteric side it is a good month to meditate on reopening your third eye. Open your channels to clearly see your spiritual goals for this lifetime.

NEGATIVE: Your temper is aroused if someone questions your honesty this month. Your blunt approach could make business enemies. You don't really mean to hurt anyone. You just tell them the truth, no matter how hard it is for them to swallow the bitter pills.

PERSONAL MONTH 9

Success and achievement is possible this month if you have laid a good foundation in the previous eight months. End projects that can be finished. Clean out your files, your closets, and your attitudes so that you can begin afresh next month with some new and exciting adventures. There is also a chance for a little romance this month if you are aware of the vibrations being sent your way. Go out of your way to do something for others, this sympathetic understanding of your friends' problems can provide a way for you to grow in human understanding.

NEGATIVE: You could become unforgiving if someone slights you. Don't turn this into selfishness or scorn; this would only detract from your outward friendliness.

CHALLENGES OF LIFE

CHALLENGES are obstacles we encounter during this lifetime. We are now concerned with the timing of events that stop you from progressing until you understand just what the obstacle is and means.

In the FIRST HALF of your lifetime, you will encounter a SUB or minor challenge which is represented by a number.

In the SECOND HALF of your lifetime, you will encounter a SUB or minor challenge which is represented by a number.

The MAJOR CHALLENGE, also represented by a number, is with you your entire lifetime until you solve the mystery. We accepted these challenges when we decided to incarnate on this planet so that we can strengthen the weak links in our destiny. Recognizing these weak links by finding the negative influences of these numbers will be helpful.

SATURN is the planet known as the DISCIPLINARIAN, the teacher, the door to the initiation and all these good things we shy away from or fear. See Saturn's other side—if you have no game going, no challenge and life proceeds smoothly straight down the road with the same scenery—where is the spice? Understand the good that Saturn brings us. Saturn is connected to the challenges of life.

FIRST SUB CHALLENGE: Subtract the number of your birth MONTH from the number of your birth DAY or vice versa.

SECOND SUB CHALLENGE: Subtract the number of your birth DAY from your reduced birth YEAR or vice versa.

MAJOR CHALLENGE: Subtract the FIRST SUB CHALLENGE from the SECOND SUB CHALLENGE or vice versa. Place all these numbers in your PERSONAL CHART on page 26.

EXAMPLE: November 28, 1951
              2   1   7
                1   6   = **1** is the First Sub Challenge
                   5   **6** is the Second Sub Challenge
                            5 is the Major Challenge

TABLE OF CHALLENGES

1—Many people will try to dominate and control your life. The remedy is choosing your own way without being belligerent about it. Know when you are right and please yourself after considering all the facts. Strengthen your self-determinism and be the daring, creative person you really are. Dependence on others can limit your talents.

2—Your feelings are uppermost and you are apt to turn others' opinions into personal affronts. This sensitivity can be very useful if you "tune" into people and see where they are. Cultivate a broader outlook on life and learn to be cooperative without being indecisive. Be thoughtful and consider the welfare of others as well as your own.

3—Social interaction frightens you and your reaction is to withdraw or become the loud overreactor. Each violent swing of the pendulum suggests that you are living in a personal construct without reality. Develop your sense of humor; try painting, dancing, writing or any artistic sort of self-expression that can bring out the real you.

4—This easy challenge is LAZINESS! However it can lead you into a rut where it is too much trouble to get out of that comfortable chair to answer the phone. Finish your cycles of activity and you will find your energy level rising. The other side of this challenge is rigidity. Learn patience and tolerance without becoming a slave.

5—This "freedom" number allows us to progress BUT it does not mean doing anything and everything we desire without paying attention to our responsibilities. There are laws of society and universe that tell us to use moderation, not overindulgence, in sex, drugs, alcohol or food. Organize your life. Recognize duties to family and friends.

6—This idealistic number may lead you into thinking that you have the best of all possible answers and belief systems. Your opinions can be dogmatic where personal relationships are at the crossroads. Do not impose your "perfection" on others. Give willingly of your time and knowledge without suppressing others' creativity. Turn "smug" into "hug."

7—This research and discovery number challenges you to become scientific and analytical. Heed your inner guidance. Develop a patience with existing conditions and make an effort to improve them. Do not stifle your spiritual nature. Your limitations are self-imposed. Cultivate faith in the justice of the general plan of things then seek to better it.

8—Wastefulness is the keyword for **8**. This can be brought about by carelessness or miserliness. A false sense of values, efficiency and judgements can become fetishes in the material world. Use your energies to cultivate good human relationships and avoid greed. Be guided by reason and not by avarice. Honor, glory, fame and money are okay if acquired in the right way.

9—This challenge is rare since it carries the lack of emotion and human compassion. It also means judging others and refusing to understand them because of an inflated ego. The time has come for this person to learn to love and empathize with others.

0—Here is NO or ALL challenges. Study all the NUMBERS above and see if you react to one. You have reached a point in your spiritual development where you can choose which challenge to release. Smooth the edges, learn and know the vibrations of the independence of **1**; the diplomat of **2**; the emotional thrust of **3**; the diligence of **4**; the expansion of **5**; the adjustment of **6**; the wisdom of **7**; the power of **8**; and the Universal Brotherhood of **9**.

If your CHALLENGES are the same as your DESTINY NUMBER, give it very close scrutiny.

NUMBERS

Every number can be expressed on three levels—
POSITIVE—NEGATIVE—REPRESSIVE. This does not mean that a
person is expressing on all three levels. You can evaluate yourself
by observing:

1. How you react in certain situations.
2. What is your chronic emotional tone?
    Happy, grumpy, short-tempered, enthusiastic,
    fearful, bored, etc.?
3. Check how the interpretations listed below
    represent your over-all response to your daily grind.

POSITIVE	NEGATIVE	REPRESSIVE
Certain	Apathetic	Despotic
Enthusiastic	Unsure	Tyrannical
Definite	Antagonistic	Suppressive
Specific	Vacillating	Hostile
Searching	Non-feeling	Violent
Transforming	Covert	Stop Motions
Activating	Resentful	Hateful

This is the reason that people with the same numbers react
differently to certain situations and differ in attitude towards
themselves and others. You can choose which level you are now
on and change your level if you wish to change yourself. You can
also change your name or a few letters of your name to bring in
the vibrations of your choice.

See our book on Name Analysis—POTENTIAL! This book
gives you an in-depth analysis of your personality. It is soon to be
available at book stores or can be ordered direct from the Rices.

Number 1:
POSITIVE: Creative; optimistic; self-determined; creative mind
through feeling; can reach a higher dimension of awareness when
preceded by a 10.
NEGATIVE: Indecisive; arrogant; fabricator.
REPRESSIVE: Tyrannical; hostile; ill-willed.

Number 2:
POSITIVE: Sensitive; rhythmic; patient; a lover; restful; a peacemaker; skilled; responsive to emotional appeal with love; protective.
NEGATIVE: Impatient; cowardly, overly sensitive.
REPRESSIVE: Mischievous; self-deluded; hostile.

Number 3:
POSITIVE: Communicative; entertaining; charming; can acquire knowledge from higher beings; inspirational; an intuitive counselor.
NEGATIVE: Conceited; exaggerating; dabbling but never really learning anything exactly; gossiping.
REPRESSIVE: Hypocritical; intolerant; jealous.

Number 4:
POSITIVE: Organizer; devoted to duty; orderly; loyal; able to heal etheric body by magnetism; works on higher levels; endures.
NEGATIVE: Inflexible; plodder; penurious; stiff; clumsy; rigid; argumentative.
REPRESSIVE: Hateful; suppressive; gets even.

Number 5:
POSITIVE: Adventurous; understanding; clever; knows the essence of life; creative mind on the mental level; traveler; creative healer.
NEGATIVE: Inconsistency; self-indulgence; sloppy; tasteless; inelegant.
REPRESSIVE: Perverted; afraid of change; indulgence in drink, food, dope; no sympathy.

Number 6:
POSITIVE: Harmonious; good judgement; love of home and family; balance; cosmic mother; self-realization; the doorway to higher mind through harmony.
NEGATIVE: Anxious; interfering; careless.
REPRESSIVE: Cynical; nasty; domestic tyranny.

Number 7:
POSITIVE: Analytical; refined; studious; capable of inner wisdom; symbolizes the bridge from the mundane to the esoteric; the mystic; able to heal spiritual gaps.

NEGATIVE: Confused; skeptical; humiliates others; aloof; a contender.
REPRESSIVE: Malicious; a cheat; suppressive to self and others.

Number 8:
POSITIVE: Powerful; a leader; director; chief; dependable; primal energy; can open third eye; money maker; sees auras.
NEGATIVE: Intolerant; biased; scheming; love of power—fame—glory without humility; impatient.
REPRESSIVE: Bigoted; abusive; oppressive; unjust.

Number 9:
POSITIVE: Compassionate; charitable; romantic; aware; involved with the brotherhood of man; successful; finisher; merciful; humane.
NEGATIVE: Selfish; unkind; scornful; stingy; unforgiving; indiscreet; inconsiderate.
REPRESSIVE: Bitter; morose; dissipated; immoral.

Number 11:   IDEALIST
POSITIVE: Idealistic; intuitive; cerebral; second sight; clairvoyant; perfection; spiritual; extrasensory perception; excellence; inner wisdom.
NEGATIVE: Fanatic; self-superiority; cynic; aimless; pragmatic; zealot.
REPRESSIVE: Dishonest; miserly; carnal; insolent.

Number 22:   PHYSICAL MASTERY
POSITIVE: Universal power on the physical level; financier; cultured person; international direction in government; physical mastery over self.
NEGATIVE: Inferiority complex; indifference; big talker—not doer; inflated ego.
REPRESSIVE: Evil; viciousness; crime on a large scale; black magic.

Number 33:   EMOTIONAL MASTERY
POSITIVE: The idealist with power to command or serve; leader who has emotions under control; constructive emotionally controlled ideas.
NEGATIVE: Erratic; useless; unemotional; not using his/her gifts of sensitivity to others.

REPRESSIVE: Power to work on other people's emotion to their detriment; riot leaders.

Number 44:   MENTAL MASTERY
POSITIVE: Universal builder with insight; can institute and assist world-wide reform for the good of mankind; can manifest his postulates.
NEGATIVE: Mental abilities used for confusion of worthwhile ideas; twists meanings of great statesmen and very able people for personal use.
REPRESSIVE: Crime through mental cruelty; uses mask of righteousness to do evil; psychotic.

Number 55:   LIFE ENERGY
POSITIVE: Abundant life; channels from higher dimensions with ease; brings light into existence; student of action; heals using life force.
NEGATIVE: Karma burdened with inaction on the right path; chooses to look backward and wallow in self-pity.
REPRESSIVE: Victim of life; in darkness; no path visible; withdraws; blames others.

Number 66:   LOVE ENERGY
POSITIVE: Self-realization through love; this love extends from self to others, knowing that one cannot love others unless one knows and recognizes the perfection of one's own soul.
NEGATIVE: Using love as a tool to enslave another; extreme selfishness and possessiveness; refusing love when time and person is correct.
REPRESSIVE: Seeing only the barriers to love; repressing loving attention to others; repressing the need to outpour cosmic love to others.

BIBLIOGRAPHY

Avery, K., *Numbers of Life*, Freeway Press

Bailey, A., *Esoteric Healing*, Lucis Pub. Co.

_____,*From Intellect to Intuition*, Lucis Pub. Co.

_____,*Initiation: Human and Solar*, Lucis Pub. Co.

_____,*Letters on Occult Meditation*, Lucis Pub. Co.

_____,*Problems of Humanity*, Lucis Pub. Co.

_____,*Telepathy*, Lucis Pub. Co.

Campbell, F., *Your Days are Numbered*, Gateway

Diegel, P., *Reincarnation and You*, Prism Pubs.

Fitzgerald, A., *Numbers for Lovers*, Manor Books

Johnson, V., & Wommack, T., *Secrets of Numbers*, Samuel
    Weiser, Inc.

Jordan, J., *Romance in Your Life*, DeVorss & Co.

_____,*Your Right Action Number*, DeVorss & Co.

Leek, S., *Magic of Numbers*, Collier-MacMillen, Pubs.

Long, M.F., *Growing into Light*, DeVorss & Co.

_____,*Huna Code in Religions*, DeVorss & Co.

_____,*Secret Science Behind Miracles*, DeVorss & Co.

_____,*Secret Science at Work*, DeVorss & Co.

_____,*Self Suggestion*, DeVorss & Co.

Lopez, V., *Numerology*, New American Library, Inc.

Rice, P. & V., *Potential! Name Analysis*, Samuel Weiser, Inc.

_____,*Timing*, F.A.C.E.

_____,*Triadic Communication*, F.A.C.E.

_____,*Thru the Numbers*, Samuel Weiser, Inc. (a series for each
    zodiac sign)

Roquemore, K.K. *It's All in Your Numbers*, Harper & Row

Schure, E., *Pythagoras and the Delphic Mysteries*,
    Health Research

Street, H., Taylor, A., *Numerology, its Facts and Secrets*,
    Wilshire Book Co.

Thommen, G. S., *Is this your Day?*, Crown Publishing Co.

YOUR PERSONAL CHART

Birthdate _____

Birth Number _____

Birth Sign _____

Birth Element _____

This planetary aspect represents the moral excellence and goodness that the soul has achieved in former lifetimes, virtues which
will assist a person in this lifetime.

Birth Musical Note _____

Personal Year for 1991 _____

Personal Year for 1992 _____

Personal Year for 1993 _____

Personal Year for 1994 _____

Personal Year for 1995 _____

Personal Year for 1996 _____

Personal Year for 1997 _____

Personal Year for 1998 _____

Personal Year for 1999 _____

Personal Year for 2000 _____

Personal Month Numbers:

January _____ __	July _____ _____
February _____	August _____
March _____	September _____
April _____	October _____
May _____	November _____
June _____	December _____

Challenges:

Major _____

1st Sub-challenge _____

2nd Sub-challenge _____

YOUR PERSONAL CHART

Birthdate _____

Birth Number _____

Birth Sign _____

Birth Element _____

This planetary aspect represents the moral excellence and goodness that the soul has achieved in former lifetimes, virtues which
will assist a person in this lifetime.

Birth Musical Note _____

Personal Year for 1991 _____

Personal Year for 1992 _____

Personal Year for 1993 _____

Personal Year for 1994 _____

Personal Year for 1995 _____

Personal Year for 1996 _____

Personal Year for 1997 _____

Personal Year for 1998 _____

Personal Year for 1999 _____

Personal Year for 2000 _____

Personal Month Numbers:

January _____	July _____
February _____	August _____
March _____	September _____
April _____	October _____
May _____	November _____
June _____	December _____

Challenges:

Major _____

1st Sub-challenge _____

2nd Sub-challenge _____

YOUR PERSONAL CHART

Birthdate _____

Birth Number _____

Birth Sign _____

Birth Element _____

This planetary aspect represents the moral excellence and goodness that the soul has achieved in former lifetimes, virtues which
will assist a person in this lifetime.

Birth Musical Note _____

Personal Year for 1991 _____

Personal Year for 1992 _____

Personal Year for 1993 _____

Personal Year for 1994 _____

Personal Year for 1995 _____

Personal Year for 1996 _____

Personal Year for 1997 _____

Personal Year for 1998 _____

Personal Year for 1999 _____

Personal Year for 2000 _____

Personal Month Numbers:

January _____   July _____

February _____   August_____

March _____   September _____

April _____   October _____

May _____   November _____

June _____   December _____

Challenges:

Major _____

1st Sub-challenge _____

2nd Sub-challenge _____

YOUR PERSONAL CHART

Birthdate _____

Birth Number _____

Birth Sign _____

Birth Element _____

This planetary aspect represents the moral excellence and goodness that the soul has achieved in former lifetimes, virtues which will assist a person in this lifetime.

Birth Musical Note _____

Personal Year for 1991 _____

Personal Year for 1992 _____

Personal Year for 1993 _____

Personal Year for 1994 _____

Personal Year for 1995 _____

Personal Year for 1996 _____

Personal Year for 1997 _____

Personal Year for 1998 _____

Personal Year for 1999 _____

Personal Year for 2000 _____

Personal Month Numbers:

January _____   July _____

February _____   August_____

March _____   September _____

April _____   October _____

May _____   November _____

June _____   December _____

Challenges:

Major _____

1st Sub-challenge _____

2nd Sub-challenge _____

YOUR PERSONAL CHART

Birthdate _____

Birth Number _____

Birth Sign _____

Birth Element _____

This planetary aspect represents the moral excellence and goodness that the soul has achieved in former lifetimes, virtues which
will assist a person in this lifetime.

Birth Musical Note _____

Personal Year for 1991 _____

Personal Year for 1992 _____

Personal Year for 1993 _____

Personal Year for 1994 _____

Personal Year for 1995 _____

Personal Year for 1996 _____

Personal Year for 1997 _____

Personal Year for 1998 _____

Personal Year for 1999 _____

Personal Year for 2000 _____

Personal Month Numbers:

January _____   July _____

February _____   August_____

March _____   September _____

April _____   October _____

May _____   November _____

June _____   December _____

Challenges:

Major _____

1st Sub-challenge _____

2nd Sub-challenge _____

YOUR PERSONAL CHART

Birthdate _____

Birth Number _____

Birth Sign _____

Birth Element _____

This planetary aspect represents the moral excellence and goodness that the soul has achieved in former lifetimes, virtues which
will assist a person in this lifetime.

Birth Musical Note _____

Personal Year for 1991 _____

Personal Year for 1992 _____

Personal Year for 1993 _____

Personal Year for 1994 _____

Personal Year for 1995 _____

Personal Year for 1996 _____

Personal Year for 1997 _____

Personal Year for 1998 _____

Personal Year for 1999 _____

Personal Year for 2000 _____

Personal Month Numbers:

January _____	July _____
February _____	August _____
March _____	September _____
April _____	October _____
May _____	November _____
June _____	December _____

Challenges:

Major _____

1st Sub-challenge _____

2nd Sub-challenge _____

YOUR PERSONAL CHART

Birthdate _____

Birth Number _____

Birth Sign _____

Birth Element _____

This planetary aspect represents the moral excellence and goodness that the soul has achieved in former lifetimes, virtues which
will assist a person in this lifetime.

Birth Musical Note _____

Personal Year for 1991 _____

Personal Year for 1992 _____

Personal Year for 1993 _____

Personal Year for 1994 _____

Personal Year for 1995 _____

Personal Year for 1996 _____

Personal Year for 1997 _____

Personal Year for 1998 _____

Personal Year for 1999 _____

Personal Year for 2000 _____

Personal Month Numbers:

January _____   July _____

February _____   August _____

March _____   September _____

April _____   October _____

May _____   November _____

June _____   December _____

Challenges:

Major _____

1st Sub-challenge _____

2nd Sub-challenge _____

YOUR PERSONAL CHART

Birthdate _____

Birth Number _____

Birth Sign _____

Birth Element _____

This planetary aspect represents the moral excellence and goodness that the soul has achieved in former lifetimes, virtues which will assist a person in this lifetime.

Birth Musical Note _____

Personal Year for 1991 _____

Personal Year for 1992 _____

Personal Year for 1993 _____

Personal Year for 1994 _____

Personal Year for 1995 _____

Personal Year for 1996 _____

Personal Year for 1997 _____

Personal Year for 1998 _____

Personal Year for 1999 _____

Personal Year for 2000 _____

Personal Month Numbers:

January _____   July _____

February _____   August _____

March _____   September _____

April _____   October _____

May _____   November _____

June _____   December _____

Challenges:

Major _____

1st Sub-challenge _____

2nd Sub-challenge _____

YOUR PERSONAL CHART

Birthdate _____

Birth Number _____

Birth Sign _____

Birth Element _____

This planetary aspect represents the moral excellence and goodness that the soul has achieved in former lifetimes, virtues which
will assist a person in this lifetime.

Birth Musical Note _____

Personal Year for 1991 _____

Personal Year for 1992 _____

Personal Year for 1993 _____

Personal Year for 1994 _____

Personal Year for 1995 _____

Personal Year for 1996 _____

Personal Year for 1997 _____

Personal Year for 1998 _____

Personal Year for 1999 _____

Personal Year for 2000 _____

Personal Month Numbers:

January _____   July _____

February _____   August _____

March _____   September _____

April _____   October _____

May _____   November _____

June _____   December _____

Challenges:

Major _____

1st Sub-challenge _____

2nd Sub-challenge _____

THE PRACTICAL PSYCHIC
John Friedlander & Cynthia Pearson

● Practical techniques for enlisting the ●
resources of your own psychic ability

"How fascinating this book is—such a practical approach to the study of our nature that one wonders why no one has thought of doing it in just this way before!"
—Robert F. Butts, co-creator of the Seth books

"This book is spirited, spiritual and down-to-earth. The authors have done their homework—and a good deal more."
—Marilyn Ferguson, author of *The Aquarian Conspiracy*

"A wonderfully clear and inspiring book, full of valuable exercises and insights. The authors succeed in de-mystifying psychic work, making it accessible and empowering to the ordinary reader."
—Roger Woolger, Ph.D., author of *Other Lives, Other Selves*

John Friedlander, a graduate of Harvard Law School, channel, teacher and member of the original Jane Roberts/Seth classes teams up with Cynthia Pearson to teach psychic development. Step-by-step instructions are provided to help you unleash your psychic ability. You don't need to possess any special talents or abilities to be clairvoyant, telepathic, or precognitive. Read this book and bring your intuitive powers to life!

160 pp. ● ISBN 0-87728-728-7 ● Trade Paper, $9.95

"What's in a name?"
POTENTIAL
The Name Analysis Book
Paul and Valeta Rice

- Want to change your name?
- Or do you want to learn to live more comfortably with the one you've got?
- An easy-to-read guidebook that explains the universal meaning of your name.

Paul and Valeta Rice explore the depths of numerology to show you how your birth name holds the key to your inner self. They explain the numbers, master numbers and the special nuances of number combinations, so you can learn to analyze your name on many levels. Without having to know any complicated mathematical procedure, you will learn how to analyze:

- your desired self and dormant self
- your special abilities number
- your karmic number—and what you need to work on in this lifetime!
- the spiritual dimensions your name holds
- the layers of meaning you can derive from your name

With this book you will be able to discover what's in a name—and if you don't like the one you have, you can change it!

192 pp. • ISBN 0-87728-632-9 • Trade Paper, $8.95

WEISER ORDER FORM

Samuel Weiser, Inc.
Box 612, York Beach, Me 03910

You may use this form to order any of the Weiser publications listed in this book:

Title	Author	ISBN	Price

Shipping and handling: We ship UPS when possible so that lost shipments can be traced. Include $2.00 for orders under $10.00 and $3.00 for orders over $10.00.

Credit Card Orders: We accept MasterCard and Visa. Call to place your chargecard order: 1-800-423-7087.

☐ Please send me your free catalog.